OLD KILWINNING

by

Roy Lauchlan MBE

Kilwinning from the Abbey Tower, 1905. The two farms at the top left and the land to the top right have now been swallowed up by housing estates.

© Roy Lauchlan, 1998
First published in the United Kingdom, 1998,
by Stenlake Publishing, Ochiltree Sawmill, The Lade,
Ochiltree, Ayrshire, KA18 2NX
Telephone / Fax: 01290 423114
ISBN 1 84033 041 4

This German howitzer was captured in France during the First World War and afterwards was gifted to the Town Council. They sited it in McGavin Park where it proved to be a major attraction to the town's children, but in May 1940 it was removed, along with most of the iron railings from the front gardens of Dalry Road, and melted down to help the war effort.

INTRODUCTION

Timothy Pont, the minister, historian and topographer who visited and surveyed most of Scotland between 1600 and 1608, referred to Kilwinning as follows: 'It doeth beare ye name Vinnen of a certane holy man so named wich came from Irland with certane of his discipells and follouers, and heir taught ye Gospel, the place of hes residence retaining still ye name Killvinnen.'

Well, what Pont stated is true. A holy man by the name of Winning, Winnen, Finnian, or something similar, did arrive at the mouth of the River Garnock, set up his church or cell, converted the local population to the Christian faith and in doing so gave his name to the area – the Cell of Winning – Kilwinning.

Little is really known about the town's patron saint, other than that he was a Culdee, a member of the old Celtic Church. We cannot be absolutely certain that he came from Ireland and the date of his arrival is uncertain. He may possibly have died in the year 715. We do know, however, that he was very well thought of, so much so that when the Abbey was founded it was dedicated in the name of St Winning and the Virgin Mary.

In 1188, Richard de Morville, son of Hugh de Morville, the Great Constable of Scotland and founder of Dryburgh Abbey, followed his father's example and founded an abbey in Kilwinning, built by one of the corporations of architects and masons known throughout the Christian world as Freemasons. These were groups established some time around the tenth century when the cardinals in Rome voiced concerns about the condition of many of the religious houses situated outwith the cities and large towns of Europe. Rural churches and monasteries were mainly built in wood and many were in a state of ruin and decay. It was agreed that a programme of reconstruction would be implemented and that all new religious buildings would be constructed in stone. To carry out this work groups of skilled artisans and architects were freed from the bonds of feudalism and permitted to move without restriction throughout Europe, building and renovating the great monasteries of the eleventh and twelfth centuries. Most of these workers were masons and as they were free, unlike most people, to move from place to place without the permission of their feudal landlord, they became known as Freemasons. It was one of these bands of masons (who set up their lodges on the site where they were working) that established the first Masonic lodge in Kilwinning.

Early lodges were in effect craftsmen's guilds and were responsible for negotiating the rates of pay and working conditions of the masons. This emphasis on trade unionism lasted until the eighteenth century at which time the movement started to take on a more social nature and began recruiting members who were neither manual workers nor necessarily associated with the building trade in any way. With this change of direction the necessity arose to have premises more suitable to new needs. The first lodge purpose-built for meetings was erected in 1779 and sited in Kilwinning's Main Street at the entrance to the Abbey Church. The second and present lodge was opened in 1893.

Kilwinning Lodge is known throughout the world because for many years it operated as the Mother Lodge, issuing charters to new lodges in Scotland and throughout the old American colonies. There was never any doubt in the town itself that its lodge was the oldest in Scotland, yet when the Grand Lodge decided to number the Scottish lodges in order of seniority, Kilwinning was only given the number 2. This did not find favour with the Kilwinning masons and they separated from the Scottish Grand Lodge and operated as a Grand Lodge on their own. In 1807 these differences were settled and it was agreed that Kilwinning was indeed the oldest lodge, but rather than alter the numbering of the lodges that had been established since the split it was decided that Kilwinning would operate without a number, hence it is known throughout the Masonic world as Mother Kilwinning Number 0.

Although the town is best known for its abbey and the Masonic connection, Kilwinning has other historical claims to fame. The ancient sport of archery is still practised and the annual pagingo shoot still attracts archers from home and abroad. The local Toxophilic Society is believed to be the oldest in the world, and there is reference to its having been in existence in 1483. The importance of the society can be gauged by its one-time patron, Prince Albert, husband of Queen Victoria, and members have included the Earls of Eglinton and Sir Thomas Brisbane, later governor of New South Wales. Other local organisations which have records of longevity are the Horticultural Society, established in 1856, and the Curling Club which has been going since 1841. The town was also the birthplace of Malcolm Campbell the green grocer, and Robert Service, the 'Bard of the Yukon', penned his first poems there.

Much has changed in Kilwinning since Timothy Pont's visit and undoubtedly many more changes will take place in the next century. Therefore it is appropriate that with the Millennium fast approaching, this book of photographic memories records life as it was during the previous 100 years.

The Green was the name given to a collection of old properties built from stones and debris from the Abbey between the mid-sixteenth and early seventeenth century. The buildings originally stood within the confines of the Abbey grounds but were demolished in a modernisation programme which was initiated immediately after the Second World War and replaced by local authority housing.

The Abbey Church, the ruins of the old Abbey and the clock tower represent more than 800 years in the life and history of the town. The Abbey, founded in 1188, represented the new dominance of the Catholic faith which replaced the Celtic church favoured by St Winning; and, in turn, the Abbey Church of 1774 was the symbol of the Protestant church which replaced the Catholic some 250 years earlier. The clock tower, completed in 1816, replaced the last remaining tower of the old Abbey which had collapsed in 1814.

To allow easier access for visitors to the town and abbey, the bridge at Kilwinning was built in 1439, but only after the Abbot of the Abbey had obtained permission from the Pope. Apart from being widened and strengthened in 1858, the bridge remains today much as it originally was.

The mouth of the River Garnock is reputed to be the place where St Winning arrived on his mission to bring Christianity to the people of Cunninghame. Legend has it that one of his first actions was to cast lines into the water to catch fish for his supper. Unfortunately, he was unsuccessful and in a fit of pique cursed the river, forbidding it to bear fish from that day onward. Fortunately for the local fishing fraternity the saint had more success with his conversions than with his curses. This 1907 view shows some of the old houses at Bridgend.

Main Street, 1905. Prior to the sixteenth century, the town's inhabitants lived mainly at Bridgend, Corsehill, the Byres and in the cottages of the numerous farms in the area; but after the destruction of the Abbey during the Reformation, the locals used stones from it to build new homes in its grounds and the centre of town gradually shifted to its present position. A close examination of many of Main Street's older buildings reveals that they were built from Abbey stone. The Eglinton Arms was a popular hostelry in the earlier decades of the century. Unfortunately a fire put paid to the business and the derelict building was eventually demolished in 1950.

A similar view of Main Street, but this time fifty years later and showing several changes that had taken place. The roadway has a modern surface and some new two-storey buildings have appeared. The shopping facilities have also noticeably improved.

The first house on the left of this photograph of Howgate became the Burgh Chambers in 1930 and is now used as the local registry and rent office.

Howgate, Kilwinning

Howgate is a distortion of the term 'Hie Gait' which translated means the 'high way' or 'high road', often the main road into a village or town. The ornamental structure on the pavement on the left is a water pump erected by the Town Council in honour of Lady Glasgow of Montgreenan who, when the newly created burgh was in financial difficulties, donated £200 to the town. The pump was eventually removed from this location during the pedestrianisation of the town centre, but in 1996, at the request of Kilwinning Preservation Society, the Irvine Development Corporation converted it into a decorative streetlamp and had it resited in the town centre.

Like many ancient towns, Kilwinning originated with a collection of small communities which in time came together as the town we know today. One of these communities was Bridgend and it was separated from the rest of the town by the Garnock. It was part of the Corsehill district and contained some very old houses. One of these was known as the 'Barracks' as it was thought that some of Oliver Cromwell's troops were once billeted there.

Dalry Road, Kilwinning

A figure closely associated with Kilwinning is the Preston-born Robert Service, 'Bard of the Yukon', who as a boy lived in the town between 1878 and 1883. Service was a poet who chronicled the frontier life in Canada and became possibly the only poet ever to become a millionaire from sales of his writing. In his autobiography *Ploughman of the Moon*, his memories of Kilwinning are perhaps a little confused as he refers to it as 'the Long Grey Town', remembering only the main street and the ironworks and coal mines in the area. However, even at this time there was much more to Kilwinning than simply one long street. Dalry Road, for example, was beginning to develop as a well-populated residential area.

The popularity of Dalry Road as an area in which to live was due to several factors such as the close proximity to the railway stations, the shops, the local school and the park. The larger mansions and villas, owned by local and Glasgow businessmen who commuted on the recently completed railways, were sited away from the town centre and mostly faced the newly created McGavin Park.

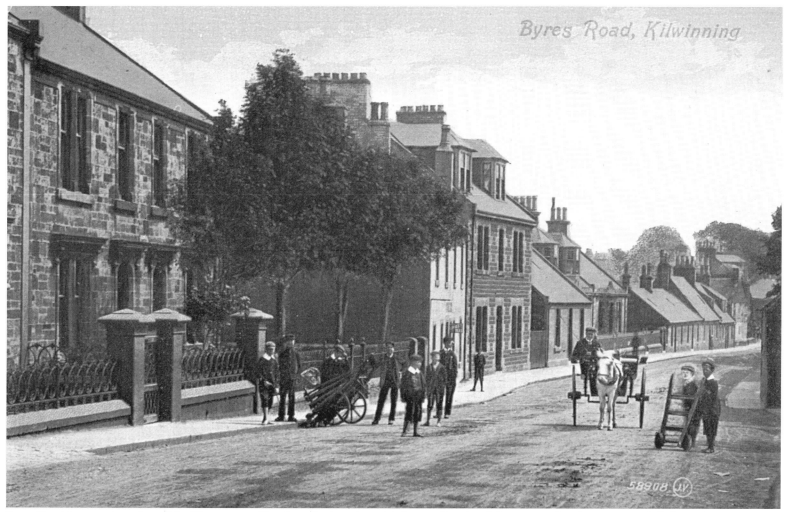

Byres Road is a continuation of the Howgate and leads to the junction of Ashgrove Road and Stevenston Road. Many people believe the road was so named because it ran past the byres of Townhead Farm; others because it passed the cattle market at the Railway Station. In fact the name is more likely a derivation of the word 'bere', a form of barley that was once grown in the area, as it was in use long before the railways arrived and the cattle markets, which depended on them, were established.

The Cross, Kilwinning

The Mercat Cross, pictured here in 1905, was at that time the last remaining example in Scotland of a wooden mercat cross attached to a stone shaft. It was originally sited in the Corsehill area before being moved to this location at the bottom of Main Street. The cross was later vandalised and since then a new one was commissioned from the New Town artist in residence, Ian Cooper.

Known as Five Roads, the top end of Corsehill was where the roads of Bannoch, Weirston, Moncur and Fergushill all met. The low buildings on the right were miners' cottages and known as Kenneth's Row, and the Star Inn, where the local pigeon breeders met, was affectionately known as the Doo Inn. The buildings here were old and sub-standard and the entire area was demolished and redeveloped.

The early 1900s was a period of great change for the working population of Scotland and while working conditions were poor in comparison with those of today, the workforce were becoming aware of their right to a better way of life. One area of change was how they spent their leisure time and this resulted in the formation of many bands and choirs. In its time, Kilwinning has been host to several bands. Some, like the Salvation Army band, had a religious connection, while others were sponsored by organisations such as the Orange Lodge. This one, the Eglinton Ironworks Flute Band, was works orientated and was one of the very first bands to be formed in the town.

The Market Bar stands at the T-junction where Howgàte, Byres Road and Dalry Road meet. The pub takes its name from the old cattle market which was sited next to the Caledonian Railway goods yard in Dalry Road. It is a typical example of a pre-war public house, complete with wood panelling, a polished wooden bar and an ornate wooden gantry. Pictured here some time in the 1930s, standing below the pub's custom-made clock, is the manager, Jackie Paterson.

Today we are used to having a varied choice of takeaways, but in earlier decades there was only one option: fish and chips. Many of the Italian families that emigrated to Scotland in the early 1900s to seek employment soon realised the benefits of the family working together and became experts in the provision of this new fast food, along with hot peas and ice cream. One of these families was Pierotti whose shop was located in the Howgate. Standing behind the his well stocked counter is Frances Pierotti.

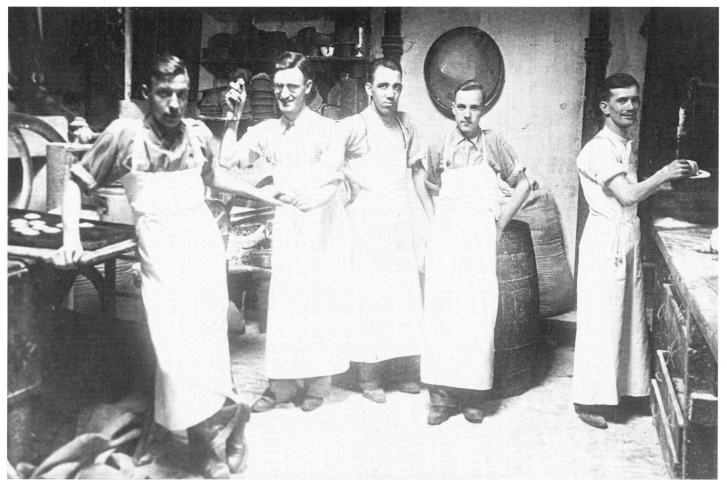

In the old days bakery items were purchased daily and consumed the same day. To meet this demand most towns supported at least half a dozen small bakehouses which also had shops. It was standard practice at that time to do most of the baking during the night so that the bread and rolls would be fresh and ready for sale when the shop opened at nine am. It was also accepted that nightshift workers from local factories could purchase newly baked rolls earlier in the morning directly from the bakehouse. This is a scene that most factory workers in Kilwinning will recall: Crawford's bakehouse with bakers Matthew Watt, John Lauchlan, Hugh Gallacher, Robert Martin and Matthew McLellan tidying up on completion of the nightshift . This bakehouse and shop was demolished in 1971.

The brethren of the Mother Lodge of Scotland witnessing the laying of the foundation stone of the present Lodge in 1892. The laying of the stone was carried out by the local MP of the time, the Hon. Thomas Cochrane, Right Worshipful Master of the lodge.

During the summer of 1947 the Kilwinning branch of the British Legion, the Town Council and the local Co-operative Society organised a gala to raise funds for an official 'Welcome Home' celebration for the local service men and women who had returned from the war. A Gala Queen, known as the Segdoune Queen (Segdoune is an old name for Kilwinning, possibly meaning 'town of the saints'), was crowned in McGavin Park and her first duty was to officially declare the Gala open. Prior to the crowning the queen was paraded through the town, accompanied by a band and decorated floats.

Pictured here is the Segdoune Queen herself – Margaret Simpson – with her six attendants, her squire and Mrs Fleming, the Provost's wife, who performed the crowning ceremony.

Kilwinning Public School, or the 'Higher Grade' as it was later better known, was originally in advance of its times. Most schools in the late nineteenth century were housed in a single large room but the plans of this one allowed for separate classrooms for the different grades of pupils. The school opened in 1876 and cost £8,097 to build. The first headmaster was John Copeland who continued on in the post from the previous school. The Higher Grade was destroyed by fire in 1971 but a new secondary school was built on the same site.

A 1940s class of Kilwinning School. At that time there was one day a year when you could guarantee that every child would arrive at school well scrubbed, hair combed and on their best behaviour – the day the school photographer arrived!

Kilwinning Athletic F.C., 1922—1923

Football is the sport which attracts the greatest interest among the male population of Kilwinning. This can easily be substantiated by the number of amateur teams supported over the years. At the very least 25 can be named. However, Kilwinning Rangers, or the 'Buffs' as it is better known, is the town's favourite team and has won no less than seventeen cups. Above is Kilwinning Athletic, another local team which brought glory to the town by winning one of the local cups in 1932.

The Home Guard was formed in October 1940 when Britain stood alone against Germany and the threat of invasion was very real. Initially, they were just a group of untrained men with no uniforms, merely an armband with the letters LDV on it – Local Defence Volunteers. By the time they were stood down in 1944 they had been transformed into a well disciplined, highly trained band of soldiers, with their officers holding the King's Commission. This is a photograph of some of the members of the Kilwinning Company of the Home Guard with their commanding officer, Captain Jack Cole Hamilton, seated at the centre.

The first postman in Kilwinning was Daniel McMillan who in the 1860s travelled daily between Kilwinning and Irvine, delivering outgoing mail to Irvine Post Office and returning in the afternoon with incoming mail for Kilwinning. Daniel carried a bugle which he blew on his arrival at the Redburn Gates of Eglinton Castle to notify the servants that he had mail for Lord Eglinton and his guests. At a later date a regular post office was established in the Main Street and the postmaster was John Service, grandfather of Robert. The post office in this photograph was opened in 1927 and remained in existence until 1971 when the present post office was opened on the opposite side of the street.

Thomas Hay's grocery was typical of many shops at the turn of the century – part shop, part dwelling house, and occupying space in a building housing another four or five families. It was the custom for the shop to be in the front room, while the living quarters were in the back room. This building is one of the oldest in Kilwinning and after lying derelict for some time it was completely refurbished in its original style in the late 1970s and now houses a Red Cross centre.

R. & J. Templeton's was one of the early multiple stores which made their appearance in towns throughout Scotland during the years between the two world wars. Quality, efficiency and competitive prices were their watchwords and staff were expected to maintain a high standard of cleanliness, in both the store and their own appearance. Today the name Templeton has all but disappeared from the high streets; following take-overs, the company name was changed to Presto and it is now Safeway.

The Winton Arms Hotel was probably Kilwinning's best known watering hole. Built in the 1820s, it provided food, overnight accommodation and stabling facilities for travellers. In later years the G&SWR railway station was built directly opposite and as it was also on the main bus route from Ardrossan to Ayr, Kilmarnock and Glasgow it was admirably suited to take advantage of the licensing laws of the time which prohibited the sale of alcohol on Sundays to all but bona fide travellers.

What became of the Clark's Spirits and Ales is unknown, but the pub was later owned by Jack Harking, a professional boxer, who was also keen on fencing and shooting. During Harding's tenure the pub became known locally as 'Hellfire Jack's'.

The Kilwinning Express ready for journey

In the years before the Second World War, when motor lorries and vans were still a rarity, the horse and donkey still had a role to play in the commercial life of small towns like Kilwinning. Commercial travellers who called regularly at local shops carried their displays in hampers and heavy suitcases, and local youngsters with handcarts would be hired to help take their samples from shop to shop. In Kilwinning this task was handled by Jim Gamble and his trusty donkey, Barney.

Kilwinning Co-operative Society was founded in 1868 and it established a new kind of trading in the town. It was run by an elected committee of local people for the benefit of the community and one service it introduced was mobile trading. As many of the town's residents lived some distance away from the shops in the centre, a fleet of horse-drawn vans visited the outlying areas selling bakery and dairy produce and fresh meats. This is one of the earlier types of van – the driver is Harry Kerr.

This van, driven by Gibby Niven, was a later model, which was the last of the society's horse-drawn vehicles.

Kilwinning Abbey owned most of the land and farms in the parish and these were rented out to tenant farmers. The Abbey also owned three mills, one of which was Sevenacres grain mill, shown here in the 1920s.

Dirran's Sawmill was the main suppliers of timber to joiners and builders in Kilwinning and Irvine. The business was owned by Neil Small and Co. who are mentioned in the accounts relating to the completion of the replacement Abbey Tower in 1816 as having 'covered' the roof of the steeple. The mill, which was located on Irvine Road was closed in 1987 and the ground sold for private development.

Eglinton Iron Works, Kilwinning

William Baird & Sons of Lanarkshire opened the Eglinton Ironworks in 1846 and in doing so became the town's largest employer. Well over a thousand people were directly employed by the company, but many others were employed by subsidiary industries on which the works relied, such as the coal mines or haulage firms which carried coal and timber to the works. The failure of the company to change from the manufacture of iron to steel resulted in the closure of the works in 1924.

The Blacklands Institute was built in 1900 by Baird & Sons to provide recreational and educational facilities for their workforce at the ironworks. It contained a library, reading room, baths and a hall for games and meetings.

The first bus services used by Kilwinning folk were established in the 1920s and run by small companies on routes that usually passed between Glasgow and Ayr and Ardrossan and Kilmarnock. This R.E.O. 14-seater bus belonged to Blanes of Kilmarnock and ran on a country service route from Irvine, calling at Doura and Fergushill and terminating at the Caledonian Station in Kilwinning's Bank Street. The driver, John Barr, is photographed here with the local postie (centre).

By 1926 most of the small companies had either gone out of business or had been amalgamated into a new company, Ayrshire Bus Owners (A1 Services Ltd). This was formed to compete on the Kilmarnock – Irvine – Kilwinning – Ardrossan service against their bigger rival, the Scottish General Transport Company of Kilmarnock. In 1930 some members of the A1 company broke away to form their own separate company and the following year this became A.A. Motor Services Ltd. This particular model, the exotically named Albion Valkyrie, was a 30-seater added to the A.A. fleet in 1932 and in service until 1941.

The Western S.M.T. Company was formed in 1932 by S.M.T. of Edinburgh and the main constituents were the Scottish Transport Company of Kilmarnock and Midland Bus Services of Airdrie. During the 1930s in particular, many smaller bus operators were bought out and their services co-ordinated into the Western S.M.T. empire. Seen here is driver George Durnie beside his Leyland Tiger, run on the Fergushill route and one of many operated by Western in the late 1930s.

Kilwinning was at one time served by two railway companies, the Glasgow and South Western and the Caledonian, both of which had their own stations and lines. The G&SWR was created by the amalgamation of several smaller companies in 1850 and mostly ran lines in Ayrshire. The Caledonian had been formed in the late 1840s but did not open a line to Kilwinning until 1888. On the left is the Caledonian station (it later came under the ownership of the London Midland and Scottish Railway after 1923), Kilwinning East, which had its passenger system withdrawn in 1932, although the station itself was not demolished until 1956. With nationalisation all the Caledonian/LMS lines were closed but those of the G&SWR were absorbed into the national network.

Porters, clerks, ticket collectors, cleaners, and the station master himself – a staff of eighteen who operated Kilwinning's G&SWR station which is still in use today.

George Mullin, a coal miner was just twenty eight years old when he died in 1931 as a result of an accident at the pit where he worked. George was also a member of the Territorial Army and as a mark of respect his colleagues there provided an escort for the hearse. The funeral took place on a Sunday to allow both mining and army friends to attend.

John McGavin was born in Kilwinning in 1816, but left the town at an early age to seek his fortune in Glasgow. He owned a successful grain business, became chairman of the Forth and Clyde Railway Company and at one time was also a Director of the Glasgow Chamber of Commerce. McGavin died in 1881 and in his will he bequeathed £7,000 to create a park in his memory, to be used by the people of Kilwinning. The park, situated at the top of Dalry Road, had an ornamental lake, tennis courts, and an area for archery practice (the lake was later removed). The Park Keeper's house in the centre of the park has recently been refurbished and now serves as changing facilities for the football and netball teams.

One of the most pleasant walks around town was on the main road which linked the two towns. On leaving Kilwinning, the road followed the boundary wall of the Eglinton Estate, the main entrance to which, the Redburn Gates, was reached mid-way along the route. Across the road stood Redburn House, which is now a hotel. The final part of the journey into Irvine was through a leafy avenue of trees and large houses. Alas, the demolition of the gates in the late 1980s and the creation of a dual carriage flyover, roundabout, hospital and housing estate has reduced the walk to just another busy road.